International Organizations

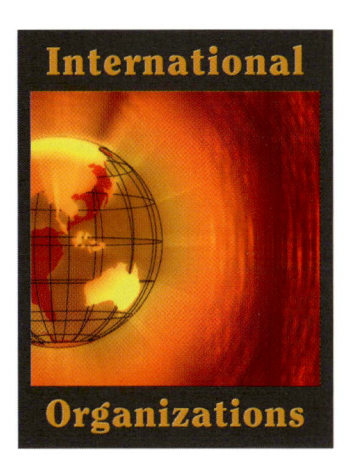

Interpol

Jean F. Blashfield

DISCARD

New Lenox
Public Library District
120 Veterans Parkway
New Lenox, Illinois 60451

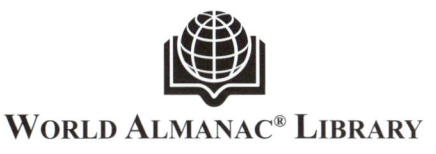

WORLD ALMANAC® LIBRARY

Please visit our web site at: www.worldalmanaclibrary.com
For a free color catalog describing World Almanac® Library's list
of high-quality books and multimedia programs, call 1-800-848-2928 (USA)
or 1-800-387-3178 (Canada). World Almanac® Library's fax: (414) 332-3567.

Library of Congress Cataloging-in-Publication Data

Blashfield, Jean F.
    Interpol / by Jean F. Blashfield.
        p. cm. — (International organizations)
    Summary: Examines the history, structure, and operation of Interpol, the world's
law-enforcement agency.
    Includes bibliographical references and index.
    ISBN 0-8368-5520-5 (lib. bdg.)
    ISBN 0-8368-5529-9 (softcover)
    1. International Criminal Police Organization—Juvenile literature. 2. Law enforcement—
International cooperation—Juvenile literature. [1. International Criminal Police Organization.
2. Law enforcement.] I. Title. II. International organizations (Milwaukee, Wis.)
HV7240.I25B58   2003
363.2'06'01—dc21   2003047935

First published in 2004 by
World Almanac® Library
330 West Olive Street, Suite 100
Milwaukee, WI 53212 USA

Copyright © 2004 by World Almanac® Library.

Developed by Books Two, Inc.
Editor: Jean B. Black
Design and Maps: Krueger Graphics, Inc.: Karla J. Krueger and Victoria L. Buck
Indexer: Chandelle Black
World Almanac® Library editor: JoAnn Early Macken
World Almanac® Library art direction: Tammy Gruenewald

Photo Credits: Interpol logo © 2003. Photos Courtesy Interpol, except the following: © AFP/CORBIS: 22; © AFP/CORBIS/Juan BARRETO: cover; American Red Cross: 34; © AP Photo/Cristobal Herrera: 15; © AP Photo/Daniel Muzio: 17; © Hulton-Deutsch Collection/CORBIS: 11; Library of Congress: 31; National Wildlife Federation: 18; © NICOLE BAGUETTE/VAN PARYS MEDIA/CORBIS SYGMA: 30; © Peter Turnley/CORBIS: 33; Reuters/Dimitar Dilkoff: 13; Reuters/Patrick de Noirmont: 5; Reuters/Romeo Ranoco: 40; Reuters/Tim Shaffer: 42; Reuters/STR: 7, 36; © Varie/Alt/CORBIS: 25; © Yves Forestier/CORBIS SYGMA: 8, 39

All rights reserved. No part of this book may be reproduced, stored in a retrieval system, or transmitted in any form or by any means, electronic, mechanical, photocopying, recording, or otherwise, without the prior written permission of the copyright holder.

Printed in the United States of America

1 2 3 4 5 6 7 8 9 07 06 05 04 03

TABLE OF CONTENTS

Chapter One	Crime that Crosses Borders	4
Chapter Two	Detectives and Delegates	8
Chapter Three	Organizing for the Work	14
Chapter Four	The Information Pipeline	20
Chapter Five	Crimes and Criminals	31
Chapter Six	The Borderless World	40
	Time Line	45
	Glossary	46
	To Find Out More	47
	Index	48

Words that appear in the glossary are printed in **boldface** type the first time they occur in the text.

Chapter One: Crime that Crosses Borders

Several police officers sat quietly in the lobby of a hotel in Luxembourg. They read newspapers, wrote notes, and chatted, pretending to be guests. They waited for a man to pick up a package that had been delivered to the hotel desk. They had received a tip that a Nigerian was smuggling **heroin** through the mail. The Nigerian man entered the lobby and walked to the desk. He asked if the post office had delivered mail for him. The desk clerk handed him a small wrapped parcel—and the Nigerian found himself surrounded by police.

The package contained a book that had been hollowed out and filled with the illegal drug. The Nigerian hadn't had to carry the heroin across European borders. He had just had it sent through the postal system.

As a matter of routine, the Luxembourg police sent a notice to Interpol—the International Criminal Police Organization—that described the crime and the criminal. A computer specialist entered the information in a vast computer database that Interpol maintains at its headquarters in Lyon, France. A database is a collection of information in a form that can be retrieved by using any of many different words. Google and Yahoo on the Internet are examples of databases made up of millions of web sites around the world.

Perhaps it was the term "postal service" or "hollow book" entered by the specialist that the Interpol computer put together with other reports. The Interpol agents soon saw that the same technique was being used in as many as thirty different countries around the world. No single hollow book could contain very much, but if all the books sent this way were added up, a huge amount of heroin was being smuggled.

There is no way that the police in any of these countries—Denmark, Nigeria, Singapore, or Luxembourg—could have discovered that a **multinational** drug ring was at work. They wouldn't have had enough information. Providing such information is the work of Interpol. Only as the twenty-first century neared had the decades-old organization dedicated to fighting international crime been able to live up to its goals.

Police in Myanmar burned a huge amount of opium, the plant substance from which heroin is made, during an Interpol meeting in that country. Myanmar authorities are working to prevent so much opium from being produced in their country.

    Interpol is a paradox—a puzzle with parts that seem to contradict each other. Many people don't really know quite what it is.

    Interpol is an international organization with countries as members. Today it has 181 members, making it one of the largest organizations of countries in the world. Yet there are no **treaties** between Interpol and its member countries as there are with the United Nations or European Union. Instead, Interpol was built privately by police officers agreeing with other officers from many countries to share information.

    Starting with a British TV adventure program called "The Man from Interpol" in the 1960s, Interpol has been glamorized so that some people think of it as an exciting body of crime fighters who go about solving international crimes. Interpol has no trench-coat-wearing master detectives. No dramatic arrests are made by Interpol agents. Peter Nevitt of Interpol told one reporter, "We're seen as a semi-mythical organization of super-sleuths. We want to get rid of the myth; we're not interested in it. Well, we like it a little, of course, but the reality is better."

INTERPOL

A Source of Information

Most countries of the world want their own police forces to solve the crimes that happen within their borders. Each country has its own system of laws. These laws decree how criminals are pursued, caught, brought to trial in a court of law, and punished.

When Interpol was being founded in the 1920s, the founders knew that nations would not agree to actually share their resources in fighting crime. Instead, they had to agree to share information.

Interpol is an information center for the world's police. The most important resource a police officer can have is information. He or she needs answers to questions: Who is that person really? Are his or her fingerprints on file? Do the police in another country want him or her? Does he or she carry out crimes that affect my country, or is the criminal activity limited to one country? Is his or her passport stolen, **counterfeit**, or genuine?

Not every person who comes to the attention of the police needs to have all these questions asked. But more and more do get this attention every year because it's so easy for criminals to travel the world.

International Crime

Domestic crime occurs within a country and is investigated by the local, state, or national police of the country. International crime involves more than

---

Interpol's Aims

According to its constitution, these are Interpol's aims.

Article 2
(1) To ensure and promote the widest possible mutual assistance between all criminal police authorities within the limits of the laws existing in the different countries and in the spirit of the "Universal Declaration of Human Rights"

(2) To establish and develop all institutions likely to contribute effectively to the prevention and suppression of ordinary law crimes

Article 3
It is strictly forbidden for the Organization to undertake any intervention or activities of a political, military, religious or racial character.

The other articles describe how countries become members and how the different bodies in the organization function.

Crime that Crosses Borders

one country. A domestic crime becomes international (sometimes called transnational) if the criminal moves across a border into another country with different laws.

Detectives in York, Pennsylvania, thought they were dealing with a simple case of camcorder theft. One of the thieves had a driver's license from Chile in his pocket. The detectives checked his name with Interpol and found that not only was he wanted for theft in several countries—and on at least three continents—but he was also wanted for murder. Interpol also provided the real names of the thieves.

Oddly, there are no international laws that define international crime. Instead, both Interpol and its 181 member nations accept that international crime is any type of crime that involves more than one nation. The criminals fit into one of three categories:

The man in the middle has just been arrested in Paraguay for a murder committed in Argentina. An arrest notice sent through Interpol gave Paraguayan police the right to arrest him.

- Those who operate across borders. They smuggle goods or people.
- Those who work in one country but whose crimes have effects in another country. Terrorists, counterfeiters, and passport **forgers** belong to this group.
- Those who commit their crimes in one country and then flee to another.

7

Chapter Two: Detectives and Delegates

Many historians think the first professional detective was a Frenchman named François Vidocq. He was a criminal who served time in prison. In 1809, the head of the Paris police persuaded the newly released Vidocq to use his knowledge of the criminal world to develop a detective bureau meant to find and arrest criminals.

Vidocq hired other criminals to be his staff of detectives. Vidocq had them make notes about the people they knew, how they dressed, how they committed crimes, and so on. For twenty-three years, Vidocq ran a bureau that came to be called the *Sûreté,* which means "security." This name is still used for France's national police force that functions beyond Paris, the capital.

In April 1914, the ruler of Monaco, Prince Albert I, invited various nations to meet in Monte Carlo for the First International Criminal Police Conference. Twenty-four nations came to discuss the possibilities of sharing crime-fighting tips with each other. The representatives decided that they would organize to share information within two years. Only a few months later, the Great War (later called World War I) began. Police work took second place to the war.

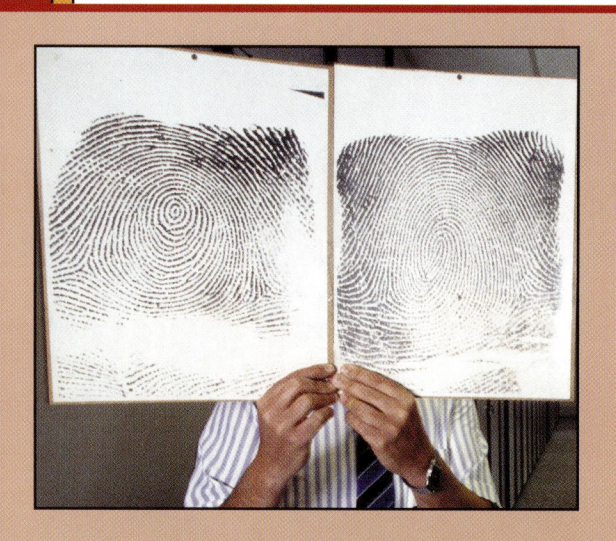

International Fingerprints

Sir Edward Henry, who became Commissioner of the London Metropolitan Police in 1903, set up a central fingerprint department at New Scotland Yard. In 1901, he invited officers from a number of countries to visit the department. Some historians regard this date as the first effort to establish an international police organization. Several years later, New York City Deputy Police Commissioner Joseph Faurot visited Scotland Yard to see the techniques in action. He brought the use of fingerprints to identify criminals to the United States.

The idea was not completely forgotten. In 1923, several years after the war ended, Dr. Johann Schober, police commissioner of Vienna, the capital of Austria, brought it up again. Delegates from twenty countries showed up at a meeting called by Dr. Schober. Remembering the meeting of 1914, Schober called the new session the Second International Criminal Police Conference. Most European countries attended, as did the United States, Japan, and China.

The delegates to the second conference confirmed the decisions made at the 1914 meeting. They created the International Criminal Police Commission (ICPC), with headquarters in Vienna. The chief of the Austrian Federal Police, Dr. Oskar Dressler, became secretary-general (the active head) of the new organization. Schober became its first president.

The ICPC was not meant to be an active police force, sending out investigators with the power to arrest people. Instead, the ICPC was to be an information center. At first, communication had to be by

Dr. Johann Schober (1874-1932)

The man who actively founded Interpol started as a policeman in the Austro-Hungarian Empire as a young man and quickly made his way into the upper ranks. As he did so, he encouraged the gathering of records on criminals of many different nations. In 1918, he was made head of the Vienna police, but just then, the treaty ending World War I split the empire into several different independent countries. He remained in the new Austria and encouraged the police to accept the new government.

In 1921, Schober was elected prime minister of Austria, but he held the position for only a few months. When he helped form the International Criminal Police Commission in 1923, the Austrian international records became the core of the new organization's criminal records. Schober was elected prime minister again in 1929 and then served as Austria's foreign minister.

Interpol communicated with its member countries by radio and teletypewriter (at the right) until recently. This photo of the radio room was taken in 1970.

telegraph and regular mail. That method was quite slow. Soon, though, radio came into use. In 1934, the ICPC developed its own radio network.

The new organization's first important task was to deal with the huge quantity of counterfeit money that was circulating in Europe. The economies of nations that were trying to recover from the Great War were harmed even further by counterfeit money. In 1929, the League of Nations (forerunner of the United Nations) assigned to the ICPC the work of fighting counterfeiting. This assignment gave the organization a legitimacy, or legal standing, that it might otherwise have taken years to earn.

Before it could truly establish itself, though, the ICPC saw that trouble was ahead. Adolf Hitler and his Nazi Party took control of Germany in 1933. Hitler put members of the Nazi party into every ICPC position possible. The German delegate to the 1935 ICPC General Assembly (the general meeting of member countries) was not a qualified policeman. Instead, he was a criminal who had spent time in prison.

In the spring of 1938, German soldiers marched into Austria and took it over. Hitler insisted that because Austrians were ethnically Germans, there could be no actual separate country of Austria. The Nazis took control of the ICPC and moved it to Berlin. Most other member nations dropped out of the organization. The ICPC records were stored in a large house in Wannsee, a suburb of Berlin. Toward the end of the war, the house was bombed, and most of the records were destroyed.

Detectives and Delegates

Within months of the end of World War II in 1945, police officers from Sweden, France, Belgium, Switzerland, and England brought the ICPC back to life. They met in Brussels, Belgium, and prepared to take up where they had stopped before the war—dealing with international criminals. Like the First World War, the Second World War left many opportunities for international crime.

The officials wrote a new constitution and moved the headquarters to Paris, France. The French volunteered to pay the organization's expenses and gave it a single small office with one typewriter. There were two staff members, including the new secretary-general, Louis Ducloux of the French Sûreté. The director of the U.S. Federal Bureau of Investigation (FBI), J. Edgar Hoover, rejoined.

The Germans who took over Austria in 1938 set up displays, such as this one in a store window in Vienna, to introduce dictator Adolf Hitler to the conquered Austrian people. The takeover changed Interpol, too.

Unfortunately, the French often treated Interpol as an arm of their own government. They did nothing to encourage the agents to respond quickly to requests for information. They didn't want to provide new equipment. But they still wanted to have a secretary-general who was French. Interpol languished under what one British writer called "the dead hand of the French **bureaucracy**."

The ICPC realized early that the police force in one country may be very different from the police forces in other countries. Some countries, for example, may have a national police force that enforces the laws throughout the whole nation. Others have community police forces and

11

Interpol headquarters in St. Cloud, a suburb of Paris, was bombed by **terrorists** in 1986. The organization remained there until 1989, when a new, ultrasafe building was opened farther away from Paris in the city of Lyon.

no national force. These variations make it difficult for police forces in different countries to communicate with each other. For this reason, the ICPC General Assembly voted in 1955 to create National Central Bureaus, or NCBs. Each member country has an NCB that serves as the point of contact between Interpol and the country's police. NCBs became an important part of the ICPC structure.

When revising its constitution in 1956, the ICPC General Assembly made several very important changes. First, it recognized that the world always referred to the organization as "Interpol." This did not start as a nickname but as the radio code name of the organization. The police group added "Interpol" to their new official name: International Criminal Police Organization (Interpol), or ICPO. Second, the ICPO incorporated the Universal Declaration of Human Rights (developed by the United Nations) into its constitution. Third, they put the prohibition against

Detectives and Delegates

political, religious, and racial matters in a paragraph by itself, always referred to as Article 3.

Even in their new headquarters in St. Cloud, to which they moved in 1966, the officials at Interpol continued to move sluggishly. Members everywhere were becoming discouraged.

Finally, in 1985, a number of countries, led by the United States and Britain, decided that it was time for someone other than a Frenchman to head Interpol. They persuaded the members of the General Assembly to elect Raymond E. Kendall of Britain's Scotland Yard to be its first non-French secretary-general since 1945. He started a "10 Most Wanted List" of international criminals, similar to the FBI's list. During Kendall's service, Interpol became an efficient organization recognized for the importance of its work.

Raymond E. Kendall (1933–)

A native of Canterbury, England, Kendall joined the military after earning his college degree from Oxford University. After his time in the army, Kendall chose to go abroad as a police officer. He served in Uganda, which was still a British colony in the 1950s. In 1962, he returned to London, England, and joined the national police force at New Scotland Yard. He worked primarily in the Special Branch, which deals with espionage and terrorism. He was sent to Interpol at St. Cloud, France, as a specialist in narcotics in 1971. Deciding to remain with Interpol, Kendall later became head of the criminal intelligence division. Starting in 1985, Kendall was elected secretary-general of Interpol for three five-year terms. The man who changed the face of Interpol retired in 2000. Kendall (right) is seen here at a meeting in Bulgaria.

Chapter Three
Organizing for the Work

The International Criminal Police Organization is controlled primarily by its own constitution. Most of the ICPO's constitution beyond the first three articles make up the General Regulations. These articles define how the business of the organization is carried out.

The work of Interpol is ordered and overseen by the General Assembly, which meets once a year. It consists of the official delegates from all 181 member nations. A new country that wants to join has to be approved by two-thirds of Interpol's active members. Regardless of its population, each member nation has only one vote in the General Assembly.

The Executive Committee carries out the decisions of the General Assembly, especially between annual meetings. It is made up of the

In 1989, a new Interpol headquarters was built in Lyon. It was designed from the ground up to be safe from terrorist attack. The building is surrounded by a wall with its entry gate arranged so that no vehicle carrying explosives can get near enough to the building to blow it up.

president (elected by the General Assembly for a four-year term) and three vice presidents, each from a different continent. The committee also includes nine other delegates who represent different countries of the world. These members of the Executive Committee are all elected for three-year terms.

Different countries take turns providing the president of Interpol. The first turn of the United States came in 1985, when John Simpson, the head of the U.S. Secret Service, was named. That year, the General Assembly met in Washington, D.C.

Jesus Espigares Mira of Spain, president from 2000 to 2004, was chief superintendent of the Spanish National Police. The three vice presidents during this period came from Canada, South Africa, and South Korea.

The American "Top Cop"

Ronald K. Noble was born in Fort Dix, New Jersey, in 1957. His mother was a native of Germany. His father was an African-American master sergeant in the U.S. Army. Noble says that thanks to his mixed parentage, "I simply won't accept that we can't work together because we come from different parts of the world or have had different experiences."

Noble attended the University of New Hampshire and earned his law degree from Stanford University. He served as chief law-enforcement officer in the U.S. Treasury Department from 1989 to 1996. In this position, he oversaw several of the largest law-enforcement agencies in the United States and became an expert on international **money laundering**. He also served as a regional vice president of Interpol. Noble left the Treasury position to become a professor of criminal law at New York University. From there, Interpol confirmed him as the secretary-general in November 2000. Noble (above) is shown during a press conference on a trip to Cuba.

INTERPOL

Structure of Interpol

- General Assembly
- National Central Bureaus ---- Executive Committee
- Secretary-General
- Standing Committee on Information Technology
- Supervisory Board for Interpol's Archives
- Financial Control
- Legal Counsel
- Police Services
  - Specialized Crimes
  - Operational Police Support
  - Regional & National Police Services
- Information Systems & Technology
- Administration & Finance
- Cabinet
  - Chief of Staff
  - Communication & Publication

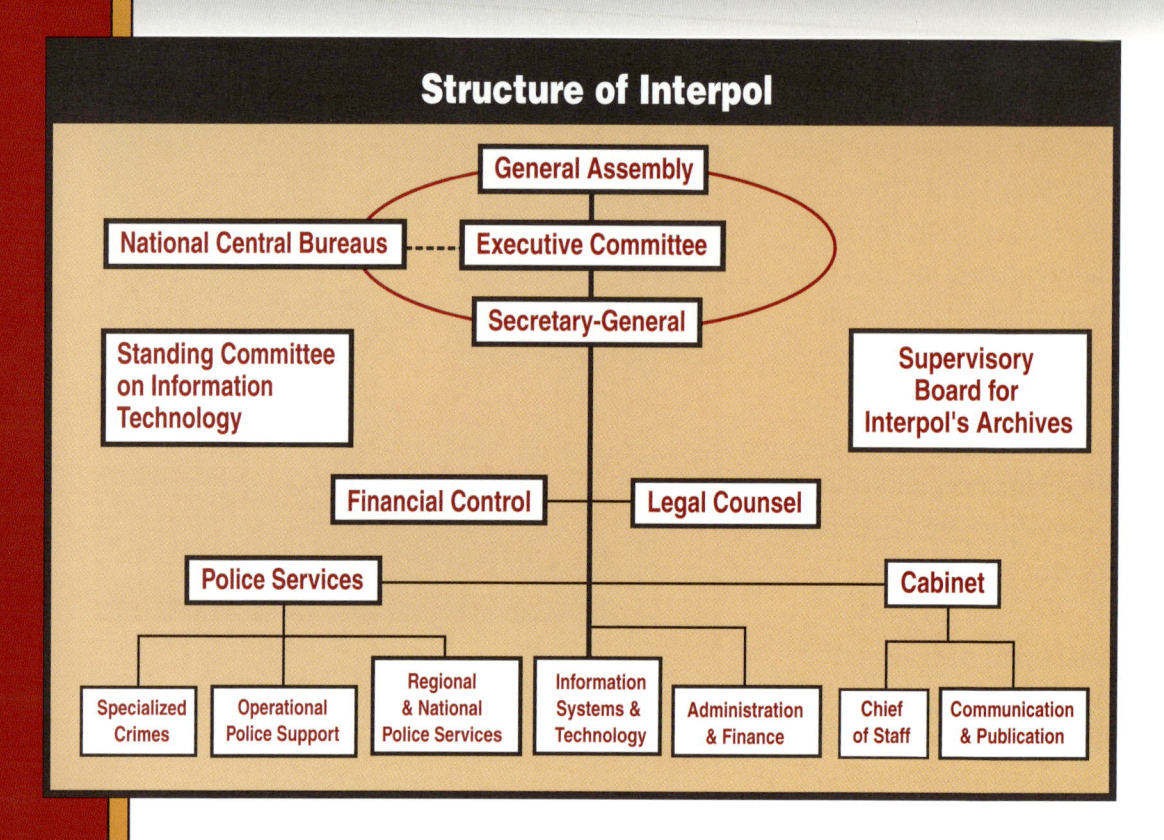

The General Secretariat

The organization that carries on the actual work of Interpol in Lyon, France, is called the General Secretariat. At the Secretariat's head is the secretary-general, who is elected for a five-year term. Since 2000, an American, Ronald K. Noble, has been the secretary-general. It is the first time an American has held the office and only the second time since World War II that the secretary-general has not been French.

The General Assembly and the network of National Central Bureaus give instructions to the General Secretariat. Interpol must not take orders of any kind from the police within a member country. Each country's police must communicate through its NCB.

About one-fourth of the staff of more than three hundred at Interpol headquarters is made up of law-enforcement agents assigned there by

Organizing for the Work

their countries. The United States usually has nine or ten agents in Lyon. The remainder of the staff do the actual work of taking in and distributing notices and developing the database that now lies at the heart of Interpol's information system.

Though Interpol does not have treaties with countries, it does have agreements with various international organizations concerned with crime. Among them are the Universal Postal Union, United Nations, Council of Europe, Convention on International Trade in Endangered Species of Wild Fauna (see box on next page), Arab Interior Ministers' Council, International Council of Museums, International Civil Aviation Organization, and Organization of American States.

National Central Bureaus

Each NCB is the point of contact with Interpol for a whole nation. No NCB can respond to a request by a member of the public, not even the

The Kidnapper and the Stones

In 1996, a trio of kidnappers in Germany held Hamburg businessman Jan Philipp Reemtsma captive in a cellar for thirty-three days before his relatives assembled a **ransom** estimated at $13 million. Two of the kidnappers were discovered in Spain living off their ill-gotten gains, but the ringleader, Thomas Drach, was not found for more than two years. An investigation coordinated by NCBs in various countries tapped the phone lines of Drach's acquaintances throughout Europe. Investigators learned that Drach, a pop music fan, would attend a Rolling Stones concert in Buenos Aires. The Argentine police were able to locate and follow him. They arrested him (right) when he returned to his luxury hotel. Drach covered his face with his shirt when he saw news photographers.

17

INTERPOL

Wildlife Crime

In 1975, a new international agreement went into effect. It is called CITES, for the Convention on International Trade in Endangered Species of Wild Fauna (animals) and Flora (plants). The following year, Interpol's General Assembly adopted a plan to cooperate in cases involving wildlife crime.

There is a great deal of profit in selling wildlife illegally. As populations of many different plants and animals are put on the endangered lists, their monetary value increases. Rare birds, such as those above, are smuggled out of their native countries, often in ways that kill them on the journey. A Komodo dragon of Indonesia's Komodo Island—the world's largest lizard—can be sold for more than $30,000 to someone who doesn't care how it became available.

Unfortunately, the laws governing the capture and selling of wildlife differ greatly from country to country. Secretary-General Kendall involved Interpol because, he said, "Extinction is final: if we wish to protect and preserve the natural heritage for generations to come, we have to act now."

parents of a missing child. The request must come through an official source. Any National Central Bureau has three main tasks. It must stay in communication with all police units in its own nation, stay in communication with the NCBs of all other countries, and stay in communication with the General Secretariat.

The United States did not have an NCB for many years. It was not even officially a member for many years. The long-time director of the FBI, J. Edgar Hoover, thought that all contact with Interpol should go only through him. Because there are many organizations within the government that are concerned with crime (see the list in the box below), U.S. communication with Interpol became almost impossible, and little was accomplished.

Finally, in 1969, after Hoover's death, the United States opened a small National Central Bureau. The USNCB is unusual for an office of the United States government in that it is controlled jointly by two different departments of the Executive Branch—the Department of Justice and the Department of the Treasury. The office is now staffed by more than one hundred agents sent to it by federal and state law-enforcement agencies. Often referred to as Interpol Washington, today the USNCB is a useful and productive organization.

Law-enforcement agencies represented at the U.S. National Central Bureau

Bureau of Alcohol, Tobacco and Firearms
Drug Enforcement Administration
Environmental Protection Agency, Criminal Investigation Division
Federal Bureau of Investigation
Immigration and Naturalization Service
Internal Revenue Service
U.S. Customs Service
U.S. Department of Agriculture, Office of the Inspector General
U.S. Department of State, Diplomatic Security Service
U.S. Fish and Wildlife Service
U.S. Food and Drug Administration
U.S. Justice Department, Criminal Division, Office of International Affairs
U.S. Marshals Service
U.S. Mint Police
U.S. Postal Inspection Service
U.S. Secret Service

Chapter Four

The Information Pipeline

A border guard in Kyrgyzstan (one of the nations formed from the former Soviet Union) is suspicious about a car that has reached a border crossing. He quickly phones his country's National Central Bureau, where an officer logs onto Interpol's vehicle database. He finds that the car was stolen from Canada six months before, so he tells the border guard to hold the driver for questioning.

Car theft seems an insignificant crime to interest Interpol, but it is an international activity of large proportions. Tens of thousands of cars are stolen each year in the developed countries. Many are shipped to and sold in Russia, Asia, and Africa. Interpol's vehicle database contains information on more than two million stolen vehicles.

The information that a country's NCB passes on is called a notice. Originally, notices were issued as actual pieces of paper that were mailed to the member countries. Today, they are largely electronic, but their purpose has not changed. Notices are identified by color, which originally was on a tab in the corner of a document.

The Red "Wanted" Notice

A Red Notice is the most important notice. It calls for Interpol's member nations to hunt for and detain a criminal. Also called an International Wanted Notice, a Red Notice means three things:

1. The offense for which a person is being sought is a crime in most countries ("a crime against common law").

2. A **warrant** calling for the arrest of the person has been issued.

3. The country looking for the person is able and willing to extradite the criminal to get him or her back.

Extradition is the legal arrangement to send a criminal captured in one country back to the country that requested his or her arrest. Extradition does not happen automatically. Most countries have special agreements or treaties with many other countries indicating that criminals may be extradited. Even under the agreement, a judge in the

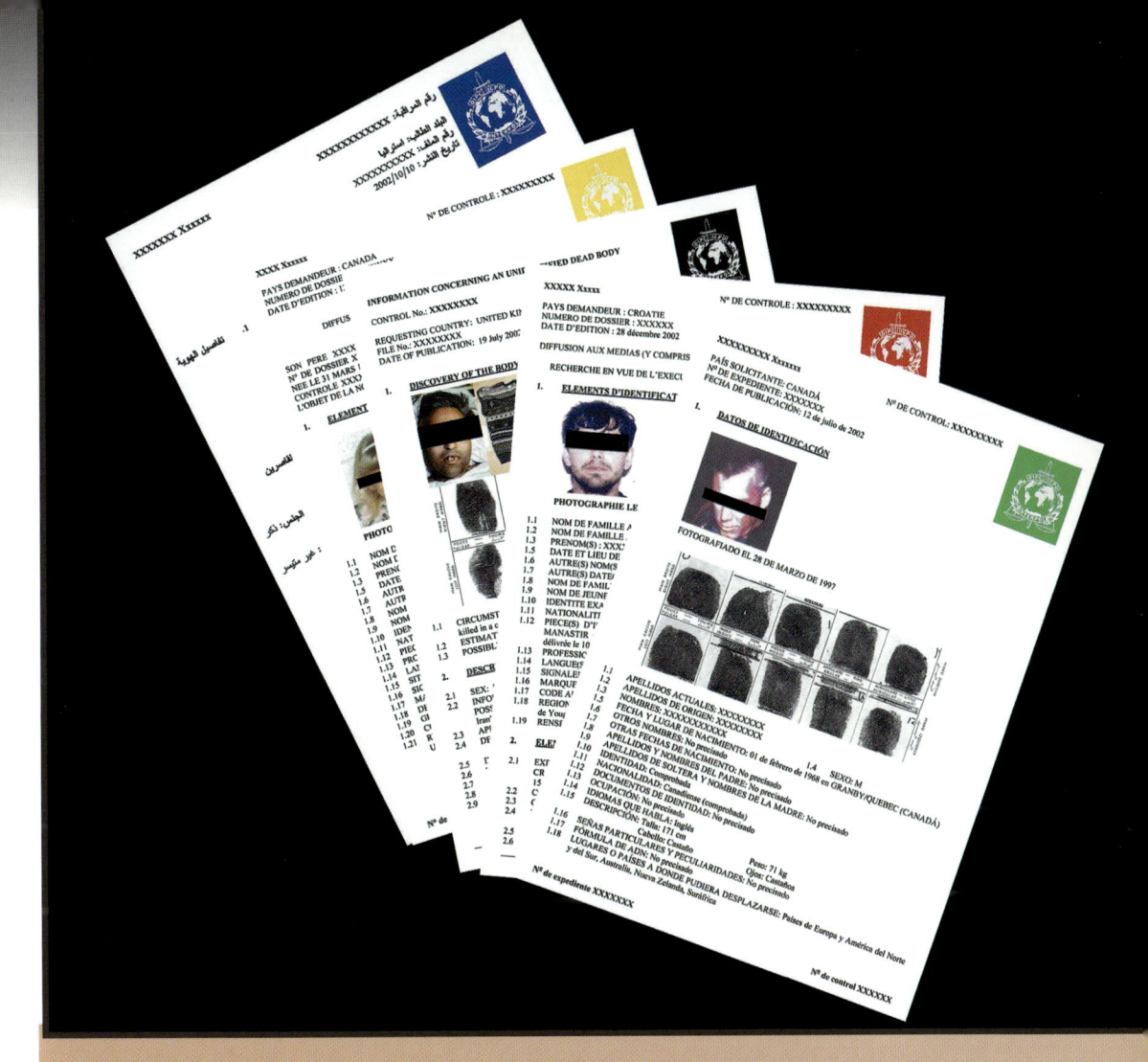

Interpol sends out five kinds of notices, referred to by the color of the tab in the corner of the paper once used. A Green Notice is a warning that a certain criminal is on the move. Red is a "wanted; pick him or her up" notice. Black concerns an unidentified body. Yellow asks for help in finding a missing person. Blue is a request for information.

country where the criminal was found has to agree that the criminal should be sent back.

Red Notices include all the information available: photographs of the criminal (both front and side views), fingerprints, a description of the way the criminal functions, his or her birthplace and date, and the status of the court case. All notices and all other Interpol communications are distributed in English, French, Spanish, and Arabic.

Wanted by Interpol
BIN LADEN, Usama

Legal Status
Present family name:	BIN LADEN
Forename:	USAMA
Sex:	MALE
Date of birth:	10 March 1957 (44 years old)
Place of birth:	JEDDAH, SAUDI ARABIA
Language spoken:	ARABIC

Physical description
Height:	1.96 meter 77 inches
Weight:	65 kg 143 pounds
Colour of eyes:	BROWN
Colour of hair:	BLACK
Distinguishing marks and characteristics:	FULL BEARD, MOUSTACHE, MAY WALK WITH A CANE

Offences
Person may be dangerous.

Offences:	COUNTERFEITING , MURDER , TERRORISM , TERRORISM CONSPIRACY , THEFT WITH VIOLENCE
Arrest Warrant Issued by:	SOUTHERN DISTRICT OF NEW YORK, NEW YORK / UNITED STATES , TRIPOLI / LIBYAN ARAB REPUBLIC

This is the Interpol wanted notice calling for the arrest of Osama (or Usama) bin Laden.

Red Notices and the World Trade Center

Soon after the horrendous attacks on the World Trade Center in New York and the Pentagon in the Washington, D.C., area on September 11, 2001, the United States asked Interpol for information about Ayman al-Zawahiri. Al-Zawahiri is known to be the right-hand man of Osama bin Laden, the leader of Al-Qaeda, the terrorist organization responsible for the attacks. Interpol sent out a query to its members. Egypt responded that it wanted al-Zawahiri for alleged terrorist activity, so Interpol was able to issue a Red Notice, allowing al-Zawahiri to be detained in almost any country.

The first country to ask for a Red Notice to be issued for Osama bin Laden was Libya in 1998. That North African nation wanted him in connection with the murder of two German citizens in Surt, Libya. Libya, which has no formal relations with the United States, would probably not have told the United States it was seeking bin Laden, but it told Interpol.

Noticing Other Colors

A Green Notice is a warning. It relays information about where a specific criminal may be headed. It helps the different police forces keep tabs on individuals.

A Blue Notice is an inquiry. It is a request for information. Before the Olympic Games or another international event, the host city may send out a Blue Notice asking for as much information as possible about pickpockets, for example. These criminals who snatch purses or cameras in a crowd are a nuisance to people who gather anywhere on Earth. With cooperation and information, the police forces try to stop such criminals at the border and prevent them from entering the country.

A Black Notice calls attention to an unidentified body. These notices are often sent out after aircraft accidents.

A Yellow Notice is sent out when a person is missing. A major division of Interpol just looks for missing children and young adults.

Lost and Found

The work of Interpol does not stop when one notice has been sent. Sometimes years pass between a crime and its solution. In 1990, a fourteen-month-old girl named Crystal Leann Anzaldi was kidnapped from her home in San Diego, California. A Yellow Notice was sent out. Seven years later, police in Puerto Rico investigating a report of possible child abuse checked the child's birth certificate and also used the Interpol database to compare pictures with another source, the National Center for Missing and Exploited Children. The abused girl turned out to be the long-missing California child. She was returned to her parents.

In another case, an American woman was traveling with a man in Europe. He returned alone with a story that she had gone on to Sweden for some health treatments. Soon, though, the woman's family began to worry. Their local police sent the information about the woman to Interpol. Many months later, in a small town in Switzerland, workers emptying out lockers at a railroad station found a bloody coat. It was taken to the police, who identified it from the Interpol notice as belonging to the missing woman. She had been murdered.

Communications

Until 1946, notices about wanted criminals were recorded in a journal, accumulated, and finally sent around the world by mail. When Interpol regrouped after World War II, the members knew they needed a quicker way to get out notices. Headquarters began to send out notices within days after they were received, usually by telegraph. Even so, it might take weeks for Red Notices sent out from St. Cloud to reach all the police forces in areas far from major cities. Criminals who were on the run had little to fear from the slow communications.

The next advance in spreading information was to use a teletypewriter, a device that translates typing on a special machine into signals that can be sent by telephone lines. At the other end, the signals are changed back into keystrokes on an automatic typewriter. This device, however, can transmit only words, not pictures. Information was sent faster, but it still was not as useful as it should have been.

The next step was the use of facsimile (or fax) machines to send out the complete wanted notice, with photos and fingerprints, by telephone lines. Many countries, though, could not afford the phone lines and other equipment. It took the computer revolution to change things.

Codes

To simplify early communications, a code was developed for telegraph that relayed a full request in only one word. The code word "ALONE," for example, meant "Please allow an officer to arrest this man." The word "BAKLE" meant "He's been placed in detention awaiting trial."

One of the most common code words was "SOPEF." This stood for the much longer: "Please send all relevant information you may possess or may be able to acquire about [so-and-so], including his or her photograph and fingerprints, details of any previous convictions, and whether he or she is a wanted person, and please let us know if extradition is or will be requested."

Identification Methods

Most of the information sent out in Red Notices has to do with identifying wanted criminals. Interpol uses any means available to identify a person. Since 1888, the law-enforcement world's main means of identification has been the fingerprint. After a century, police began using Automatic Fingerprint Identification Systems, or AFIS, to automatically compare prints. Interpol has been using the FBI's AFIS system in recent years. Because many criminals from around the world come to the United States at some time, the FBI files are very useful for Interpol. The FBI has more than 250 million sets of fingerprints in its automated files, and the files grow every day. Not all of the fingerprints belong to criminals; many are those of people in military and other government jobs.

The use of electronic equipment to identify people is called biometrics. In biometrics, a device using radio waves measures the pattern in the layer of skin beneath the surface and compares it with the original fingerprints. This is a quicker and more accurate process than using a human to compare prints.

The iris of the eye is also a biometric identifier. The colored circle in the eye consists of many different colors

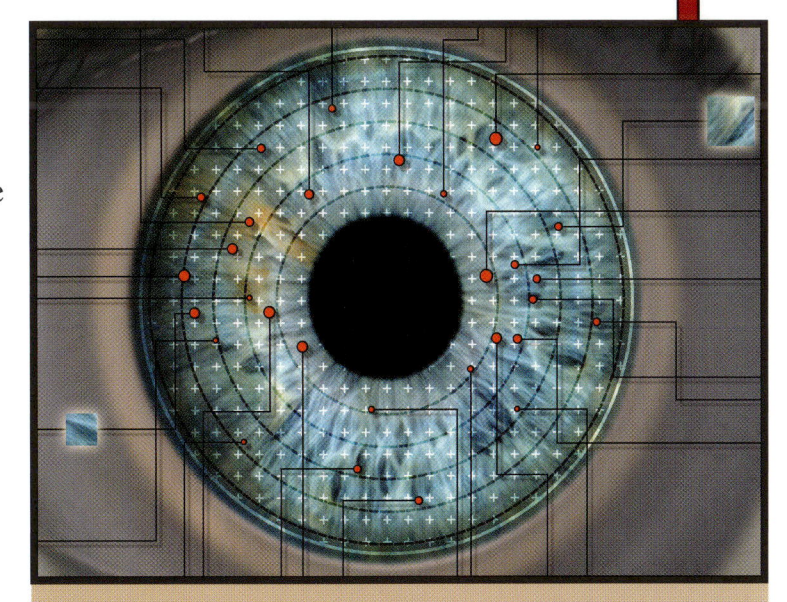

When the iris of a person's eye is scanned and a computer recording is made, many specific points of color—which do not change during the person's life—can be recorded.

INTERPOL

and specks. When biometric equipment scans an iris, it records 266 points of color or light or dark specks in the iris. Then it creates a mathematical equation based on those points. Many years later, a person's iris might be measured again, and he or she can be identified if the system locates at least 150 of the points that appear in the equation.

Another biometric identifier is DNA (deoxyribonucleic acid). DNA is the genetic chemical in the body that determines an individual's characteristics. As far as is known, this chemical is different in every person on earth. It can be analyzed from a hair, flakes of skin, spit, or semen. The exact DNA information can be converted into a bar code, similar to the universal bar codes on products in stores. This bar code can be sent by computer anywhere in the world so it can be compared with a sample from a person who has been arrested. Interpol calls the use of DNA "one of the most significant developments in the ability of the police to detect crime from evidence left at the scene."

Interpol is working on many means of identification for the future. For now, classic photographs and fingerprinting remain the basic tools, along with calling attention to other peculiarities, such as an odd limp. Perhaps a criminal has an unconscious habit of rubbing his left ear when he's lying, or maybe she bites her fingernails. Any such information may be useful in apprehending that criminal.

The Switch to Computer

With the development of a global communications network, Peter J. Nevitt, director of Interpol's information and technology department, brought Interpol into the twenty-first century. Nevitt has been described as the "enemy of all the world's thugs." Today, because of his work, notices and other communications move nimbly by e-mail over networks that are as secure from outside interference as possible.

Not all nations are yet computer savvy, but Nevitt and Secretary-General Noble plan for that to happen as soon as possible. The United

Peter J. Nevitt, "the enemy of all thugs," has used his knowledge of computers and criminals to develop today's Interpol's swift communication and database systems.

States and other wealthy countries are donating computer equipment to developing nations.

Interpol uses two kinds of communications. First, one country's police can correspond directly with the police of another country by sending notices through the e-mail network. Second, any member country can connect directly into Interpol's vast databases.

One of the things that used to slow up Interpol communication was the fact that the headquarters could be reached only eight hours a day, Monday through Friday. Crime doesn't only happen during business hours. When Ronald Noble took over as secretary-general, he changed the work hours at Interpol to make the organization's communications function twenty-four hours a day, seven days a week. A computer-wise language specialist is on duty at all times to receive, translate, and send notices on their way. Noble pictures the law-enforcement officer of the future as "someone who is as adept in stopping computer-related crime as in stopping violent crime. Someone who's as comfortable at a PC terminal as he or she is at a firing range."

27

INTERPOL

Information Databases

When information was first being gathered and organized by Interpol, it consisted of paper files that had to be stored. If a country requested a search, clerks had to go through all the files to find the information. This process might have taken days. There were more than four million records, which took up a lot of space. Clerks sat in chairs mounted on rails so that they could slide back and forth along the file cases. The records had to be continually updated and catalogued, a horrendous but vital task. Today, the Interpol database—called the International Criminal Information System, or ICIS—is fully computerized. It can be searched in just minutes.

How is the system used? One of Interpol's main activities is to serve as a communications center involving crime that crosses borders. Suppose

Until recently, the millions of records at Interpol had to be sorted, studied, and filed as individual pieces of paper. It became an impossible task to keep up with the work, even though the clerks slid back and forth on tracks, as seen here in this 1970 photo of the record room at St. Cloud.

The Information Pipeline

a mysterious person—Mr. X—comes to the attention of police in California. They think he might be involved in crime, but they can't find any local police records on him. Before they let him slip out of sight, they contact USNCB by computer with an inquiry: Do they know, or can they find out, anything about this Mr. X?

The Washington office contacts Lyon, where Interpol checks its own database. If they find nothing, they send out a notice to the NCBs of all member nations. A reply comes from Thailand saying that the presence of Mr. X was noted when large quantities of illegal drugs were being moved through Thailand to Taiwan. At that time, however, the Thai police did not have enough evidence to hold Mr. X. The California police decide to keep a quiet eye on Mr. X to see what he might be up to.

Not all countries can obtain information from all other countries. Some of them do not have treaties with each other that allow them officially to work together. The computerized database system was designed to take care of this problem. If country A is not on official good terms with country B, an Internet search by country B will not provide any information from country A.

Databases on the Web Site

Some of the information held by Interpol's databases is available to the public by computer. The public can log on to www.interpol.int, the official Interpol World Wide Web site. Click

---

Keying in the Criminals

The following information may be recorded in the Interpol database entry about a specific criminal.
- Date fingerprinted
- Reason fingerprinted
- Fingerprint classifications
- True identity
- Aliases
- Maiden name
- Date of birth
- Height
- Weight
- Hair color
- Languages spoken
- Marks on skin
- Occupation
- Type of offense

DNA information will be added gradually as it becomes available.

INTERPOL

Helping police forces find missing children has been an important part of Interpol's work since the beginning. This paper Green Notice showing photographs of many missing children was send out by Interpol in the early 1990s when a child killer was active in Europe.

"Wanted," and you can see some—but not many—of the fugitives wanted by police forces around the world. On a day in early 2003, among the pictures and various personal details given were data on a Dutch man wanted in the United States for drug dealing, a kidnapper wanted in India, a murderer wanted in Libya, and a German wanted in Monaco for **fraud**. A similar section on the web site shows photos of some missing children. Interpol encourages police and the public to check the site often in the hope that the children may be recognized.

Part of the Interpol web site can be reached only by authorized law-enforcement officers. This part may contain information that would be helpful to criminals if it were made available more widely.

Crimes and Criminals

Chapter Five

In the early days, Interpol's primary work involved chasing murderers, counterfeiters, and robbers across international lines. Today, the crimes they investigate have changed to ones that are international by their very nature. Interpol has specialized crime groups that work in five areas: public safety and terrorism, fugitives, organized crime and drugs, financial and high-tech crimes, and trafficking in human beings.

Terrorism

Terrorist acts can kill people of any nationality at any time anywhere. When Interpol was reformed after World War II, Article 3 was added to the organization's constitution. It says that Interpol must not concern itself with "activities of a political, military, religious or racial character." That decision caused trouble.

In March 1950, some Czechoslovakians took over two aircraft and forced the pilots to fly them to that part of Germany controlled by the United States after the end of World War II. The men requested political asylum, which meant that they were asking to be allowed to stay because they were in danger at home for political reasons.

The Czech government called the men criminals and issued a Red Notice through Interpol. Interpol followed its normal procedure and issued the notice. J. Edgar Hoover, the head of the FBI, pulled the United States out of Interpol. He said that the organization should not have issued the notice because it was a political issue, not a criminal one.

J. Edgar Hoover began to build the FBI into an important law-enforcement body when he was a young man.

INTERPOL

Carlos the Jackal

He began in the 1970s as a terrorist, killing to call attention to the plight of the Palestinians. He ended up as an ordinary wanted criminal who was finally captured by the French in Sudan in 1994. Known as "Carlos" to the Popular Front for the Liberation of Palestine, he was really a Venezuelan named Ilich Ramirez Sanchez. He acquired the nickname of the Jackal after a copy of Frederick Forsyth's novel *The Day of the Jackal* was found on a bookshelf in an apartment he rented in London. As the Jackal, Ramirez Sanchez may have been involved in the massacre of Israeli athletes at the 1972 Munich Olympics. He may also have masterminded the taking of hostages at the Vienna meeting of the Organization of the Petroleum Exporting Countries (OPEC) in 1975. Paid for by Libya, the hostage-taking left three dead. Some hostages were flown to Algeria, where they were released, and Carlos was given asylum.

After he was expelled by the Popular Front for not following orders, Carlos developed his own terrorist organization. His skills were available to anyone who had the money to pay him. His organization may have been responsible for at least eighty murders over the years. After he was captured in Sudan, he was taken to France and tried for the 1975 murders of two French policemen and a police informer. During the trial, however, he revealed himself not as a terrorist working to help the cause of Palestine independence but as a thug who was against everything except the pleasure of being widely recognized as an important criminal.

Czechoslovakia and several other communist nations in Eastern Europe also resigned from Interpol.

Unfortunately, this episode caused Interpol to shy away from all involvement in possible terrorist acts for several decades. The United States did not officially rejoin Interpol for twenty years, although Interpol continued to use FBI records.

It has been said that "one man's terrorist is another man's freedom fighter." Interpol members spent years trying to define terrorism to the satisfaction of all. Not even the United Nations has been able to agree on a definition. Even without defining terrorism, however, Interpol fights it.

As the years passed, however, more murders, kidnappings, and other crimes were being carried out by people who claimed they were freedom fighters, that they were escaping political oppression, or that they were

Crimes and Criminals

trying to "liberate" a people or call attention to the plight of some prisoners somewhere. At the 1984 General Assembly meeting in Luxembourg, Interpol members decided that destructive actions carried out by terrorists are actually crimes regardless of the reason for them.

The United States Rejoins

On October 7, 1985, an Italian cruise ship, the *Achille Lauro*, was in the eastern Mediterranean. Many of the four hundred passengers and crew got off in Cairo, Egypt, to visit the pyramids. The ship went on to Port Said, where the passengers would rejoin it. Suddenly, off the coast of Egypt, terrorists belonging to the Palestine Liberation Front hijacked the ship and held ninety-five remaining passengers and crew hostage. They demanded that Israel release fifty Palestinian prisoners.

For two long days, the world watched. When the nation of Syria turned down the hijackers' request to go there, one hijacker took out his anger on an elderly wheelchair-bound passenger, an American Jew named Leon Klinghoffer. He was shot, and his body and his wheelchair were shoved overboard. This event was not known, though, until Egypt agreed that the hijackers could go free if they released the passengers. The United

Egyptian soldiers guard the cruise ship *Achille Lauro* at Port Said, where it docked after it had been hijacked by terrorists and held for two days in 1985. The hijackers killed one elderly American passenger.

Construction workers labored for many months after September 11, 2001, removing the ruins of the World Trade Center, destroyed by airplanes that had been hijacked by terrorists.

States asked Interpol to issue warrants for the kidnappers' arrests. The Egyptians were attempting to fly the hijackers out of the country when a U.S. fighter plane forced their aircraft down in Italy. The Italians, responding to the Interpol Red Notice, took the hijackers into custody. The Italians refused to arrest the leader of the hijackers at first, and then he left the country. U.S. troops captured him in Iraq in 2003.

The episode of the *Achille Lauro* changed opinion in the United States in the 1980s. The United States began to issue warrants through Interpol in response to other terrorist acts. By doing so, it acknowledged Interpol's importance in fighting terrorism.

Interpol left Article 3 in its constitution but began to interpret it differently. To deal with terrorism, a specialist unit was created to look at crimes in terms of what was done, not why. Ronald Noble wants Interpol to become the central clearinghouse of information that plays a role in terrorism. This includes everything from stolen passports and credit cards to **money laundering**, arms sales, and kidnapping.

Crimes and Criminals

Just before the 2002 General Assembly meeting in Cameroon, terrorists bombed a popular nightclub on the Indonesian island of Bali. More than two hundred people, mostly Australians, were killed. The members of the General Assembly immediately voted to increase the budget for fighting terrorism.

Organized Crime

Many different kinds of crime are carried out by organizations of criminals. Interpol considers organized crime a major concern because it touches all of Interpol's activities. Organized crime controls most of the **drug trafficking** of the world. The money the organizations take in affects the economy of every nation. Also, organized crime groups are willing to use violence to achieve their goals.

To Americans, "organized crime" usually means the Mafia, which has controlled crime in major U.S. cities since the days of Al Capone and still does to some extent, but organized crime is found everywhere. The Italian Mafia (both in Italy and the United States), the Yakusa in Japan, South American drug **cartels**, and the recently exposed Russian Mafia are among the largest criminal organizations.

Most European countries are participating in Interpol's Millennium Project, which is gathering information about the organized gangs from the former Soviet Union. It is estimated that since the collapse of the Soviet Union, about a thousand Russian organized crime groups have been operating internationally. Eight or ten times that many are operating in the former Soviet countries. They are involved in such crimes as cigarette

Massive Money Laundering

The United Nations estimates that the trade in illegal drugs each year is larger than the entire world's oil and gas industry. At least half of the money that changes hands for drugs is laundered through the electronic funds transfer system of the world's banks. About seventy thousand money transfers take place every day, totaling about $2 trillion. Money launderers have no problems tucking their funds into the system, and the money can't easily be traced.

INTERPOL

and drug smuggling, illegal immigration, **extortion**, **prostitution**, vehicle theft, and arms dealing. Many countries want to see them stopped.

No matter where organized crime functions, one of the biggest problems the criminals face is dealing with the money that has been obtained illegally. They must make it appear legitimate, or lawful, if they are going to spend it. This process, called money laundering, usually involves the transfer of funds by computer, called electronic funds transfer. When money is moved from one country into another, the first country cannot go after it. That's where Interpol comes in.

It's been estimated that organized crime the world over makes $1.5 trillion dollars a year. Almost half of that is laundered in some way.

Crimes of Art and Mind

Thousands of pieces of art are stolen every year, especially in European countries. There has always been a market for stolen art. Some buyers don't ask where a painting or sculpture came from—they just want it. By clicking on "Works of Art" in the Interpol site, art buyers can now see some of the art objects that have been reported missing around the world. Interpol has also prepared a CD-Rom showing art objects

An official shows a seventeenth-century Dutch still-life painting that was stolen from a museum in Ukraine. Police in England located the painting based on Interpol information.

36

Crimes and Criminals

that have been missing through the years. Showing about twenty thousand missing art objects, the CD-Rom is intended for use by auction houses, antique dealers, museums, and even art lovers in general. In addition to paintings and sculpture, it covers many other categories, such as furniture, weapons, musical instruments, religious items, books, and even mummies. Interpol estimates that the illegal trade in art and cultural objects worldwide may amount to $4.5 billion every year.

Another category of art-related crime is the piracy and counterfeiting of films, music CDs, and even high-priced designer clothing and handbags. This is called the theft of intellectual property. Producers of films and CDs lose money when their products are copied, or counterfeited, in other countries and distributed as if they were legitimate. When money is lost that way, there is less money available for the original producers to create later products.

Ronald Noble says that it is "right for Interpol to assist not only in investigating and prosecuting the people who do this, but in sharing information about how the counterfeiting occurs, what counterfeiting networks are used and getting that information out on the Internet to police agencies." In 2000, the General Assembly agreed and started to develop specialists in intellectual-property crimes.

The Smuggling of People

Smuggling—or the movement of goods across a border illegally—has always been a common international crime, but people smuggling is a more recent phenomenon. Many people who are unemployed or feel in danger from a government want to enter another country such as the United States. Because they know they could never enter legally, they may pay a large amount of money to a smuggler to sneak them in. Often, once the smuggler has the money, he allows terrible things to happen to the people being smuggled. More than once, ships have docked bearing the dead bodies of people locked in giant shipping crates.

INTERPOL

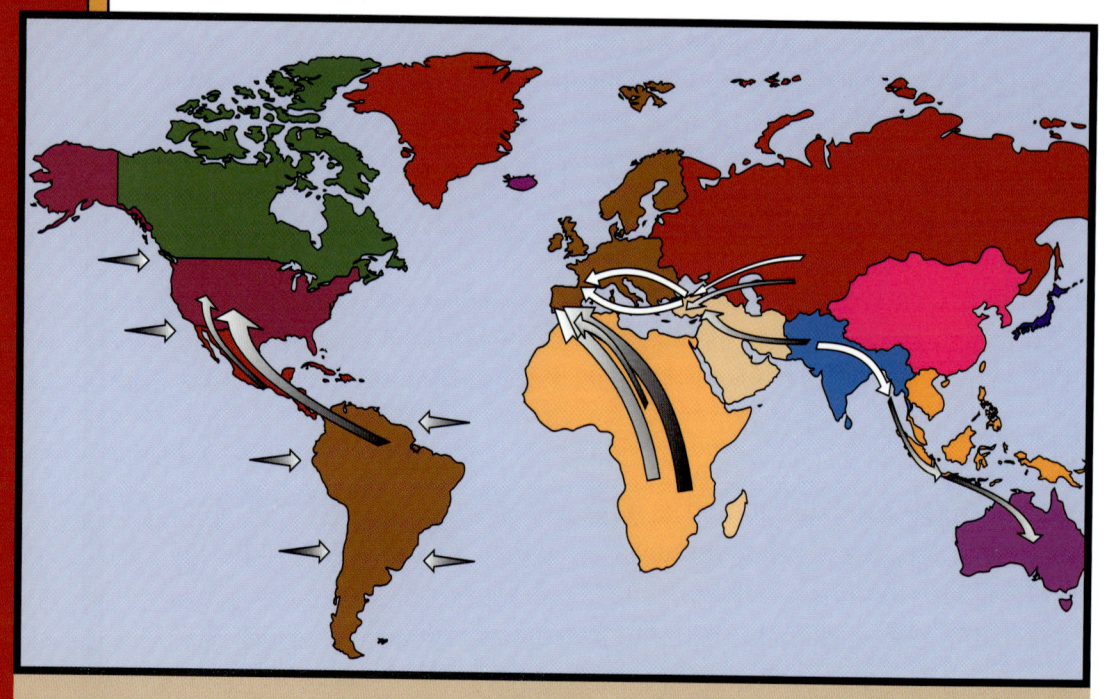

The arrows on this map trace some of the world's major people-smuggling routes.

Illegal immigrants from China have suffered greatly and often died in the attempt to enter other countries. Sometimes they had been traveling for weeks. In 2000, British authorities found a truck on a ferry from the Netherlands that contained the bodies of fifty-eight Chinese people who had tried to be smuggled in but died in the attempt. At about the same time, twenty-five Chinese men were found alive in a container aboard a ship in Vancouver, British Columbia.

In 2001, a rusting ship was deliberately run aground on the coast of southern France. It was found to be carrying 894 illegal immigrants, about half of them children, who were starving and sick. Each one had paid up to $2,000 for the journey. The ship, which had sailed from Turkey, was carrying Kurdish people. The miserable travelers had had

Crimes and Criminals

no way to clean themselves during the journey. The captain and crew disappeared, but the immigrants were allowed to apply for asylum.

In 2002, a freight car on a sidetrack in Iowa was found to contain the bodies of eleven Mexican and Central American adults. They had probably been locked inside the freight car by a smuggler, perhaps a long-time smuggler called Hernandez. He abandoned the people, who then died of heat and starvation.

Interpol started Project Bridge in 1999 to collect information on organized smuggling groups and to improve ways for nations and the international community to fight the smuggling of people.

Counterfeit Money

One of the main reasons Interpol was formed was to help police forces deal with the problem of counterfeit money, which is often distributed from one country to another. Today, eighty years later, counterfeit money from countries with strong economies is still one of Interpol's primary concerns. Banks, customs officials, and other people who deal with currency have access to Interpol's database and its publication, *Counterfeits and Forgeries Review*, which has provided police with examples of real and counterfeit currencies since 1923. The Interpol expert shown here is inspecting recently discovered counterfeit currency.

More and more people the world over are using credit and debit cards—"plastic money"—instead of currency, and fake cards are now being manufactured. Interpol is prepared to take on the task of helping police forces, banks, and retailers identify these counterfeits, too.

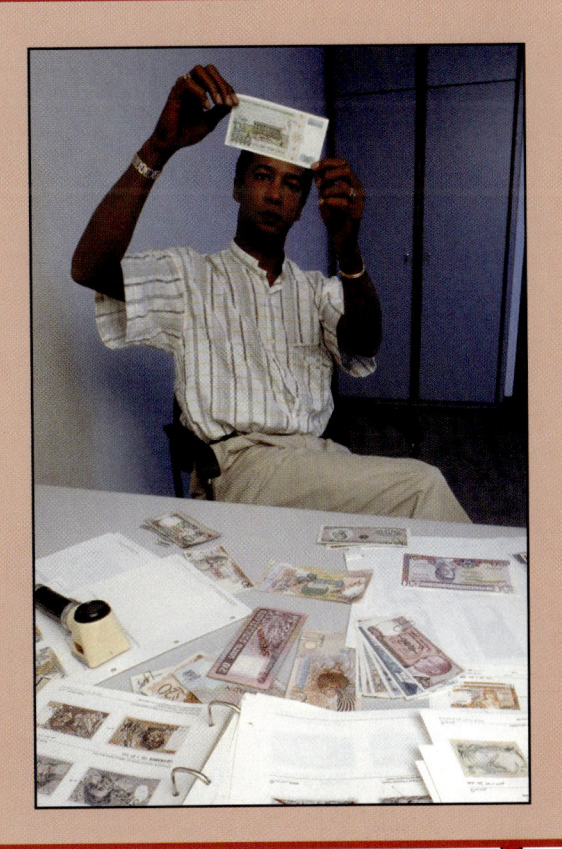

Chapter Six: The Borderless World

The world that exists today is very different from the one in which the International Criminal Police Organization was founded. Through most of the twentieth century, crime has become increasingly **globalized**. With its new technology and attitude, Interpol is likely to play an important role in fighting crime in the twenty-first century.

Patrolling the Internet

Before leaving office in 2000, Secretary-General Kendall called the attention of the law-enforcement agencies of the world to the problem of crime involving the Internet, or "cybercrime," as he called it. Kendall said, "I think everybody was taken by surprise by the speed and explosive nature of the development [of cybercrime]. Here we are faced with a new phenomenon, and a phenomenon that has already developed very, very quickly. That means that the response ought to be developed quickly as well."

One of the major problems is that there are no precedents, or laws written earlier, that deal with cybercrime. When Onel de Guzman was found to have sent a virus called ILOVEYOU around the world from the Philippines,

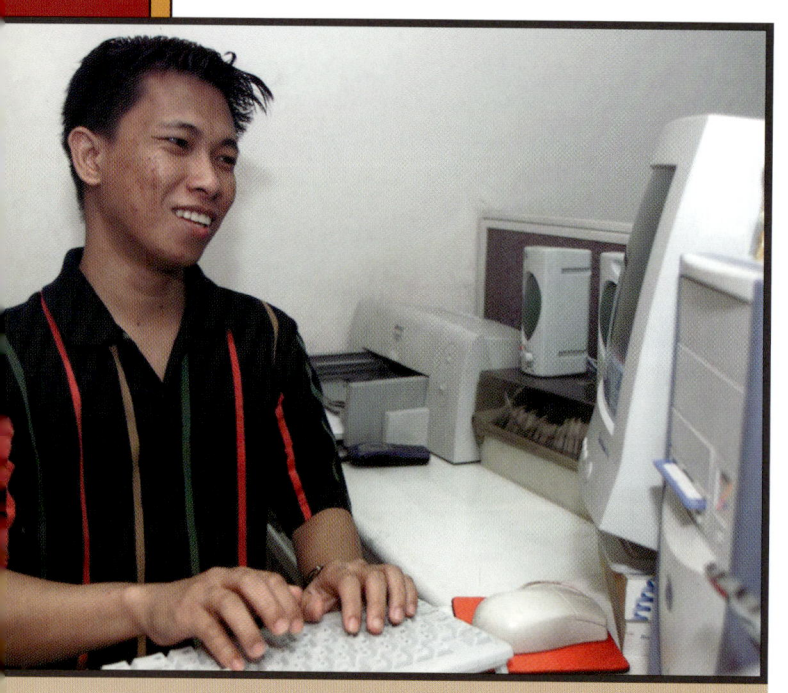

The world realized that there was a new kind of crime in 2000 when this young Philippine man, Onel de Guzman, created a computer virus called ILOVEYOU that affected businesses around the world.

40

there was no law under which he could be charged. The virus affected computers around the world and cost businesses millions of dollars to fix. Guzman was finally charged with the illegal use of a credit card.

Kendall said, "If we waited until the laws were adopted, we would wait a long, long time. Unless we have the courage to step outside the usual run-of-the-mill responses, we will not achieve anything." In 2003, Secretary-General Noble persuaded the General Assembly to increase Interpol's budget. It will finally have the money to function the way it should. Interpol should be able to anticipate crime, not just react to it.

To Act or Not to Act

Many countries regard a Red Notice as legal justification to arrest someone. The United States, though, will arrest someone on a Red Notice only if the United States has an extradition treaty with the country that posted the notice. This is primarily because many countries do not have justice systems that the United States regards as fair.

On the other hand, some countries do not believe in **capital punishment**. Such countries will not extradite people wanted in the United States for murder if they are likely to be executed.

Months after the girlfriend of Ira Einhorn, a well-known hippie in Philadelphia, had disappeared from view in 1977, her body was found in his apartment, wrapped in Styrofoam. Just before his trial in 1981, Einhorn escaped. The trial was held anyway, and he was convicted of murder *in absentia* (in his absence). The United States NCB sent out a Red Notice on Einhorn, but he disappeared for almost twenty years.

Einhorn was finally located through the work of Interpol, which had never stopped looking for him. The killer's Swedish wife, Anika, had applied for a driver's license in France. On the application, she used her real name. Interpol's database was routinely checked. It showed that she might be related to Einhorn. The French police thus had his address, and he was arrested in July 2001, but the French refused to extradite him

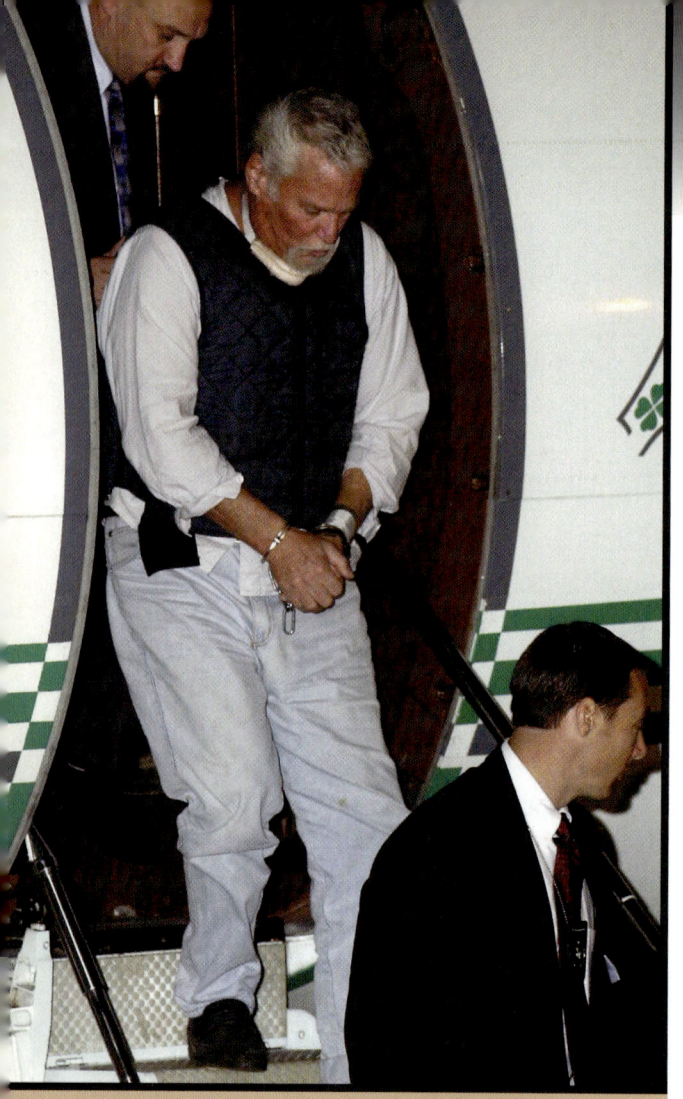

After living in Europe as an escaped criminal for twenty years, Ira Einhorn was arrested in France and brought back to the United States. He is serving a life sentence in prison for murder.

because he might be executed in the United States. They set him free.

A major diplomatic struggle between American authorities and French human-rights advocates went on for months. The French finally gave in, and Einhorn was rearrested. In a dramatic protest, Einhorn cut his throat with a kitchen knife while reporters watched. The cut did little damage and didn't change anything for him—he was brought back to the United States. He was retried, and at the end of 2002, he was found guilty of murder. The hippie killer was sentenced to life in prison.

Terrorism and the Future

The twenty-first century is starting off as an age of terrorism. Interpol is gearing up to play an important role in preventing terrorist acts. Since the terrorist acts of September 11, 2001, nations the world over have sought to keep better track of the people who enter their countries.

Secretary-General Ronald Noble, in a speech in 2003, said, "One cannot escape the impact that terrorism, in its many forms, has had on our member countries and on police and security forces worldwide. No matter what any of us might have thought before September 11, 2001,

The Borderless World

terrorism instantly became our Number One global priority on that date. Whether we live in Africa, the Americas, Asia, Europe or the Middle East, the number of terrorist incidents accompanied by graphic images witnessed by us since the September 11 attacks, and indeed over the last year in places like Bali, Kenya, Colombia and Pakistan, should make each of us feel that terrorism could indeed strike any of our countries, organizations or colleagues anywhere in the world at any time. When Interpol thinks about criminality, terrorism, and security, our principal concern is people—the actual populations of target countries."

New technology will allow the names of foreigners entering the United States, for example, to be instantly checked against Interpol's database of crimes committed overseas. Their passports will be checked against international databases—instead of just American ones—to see whether they were stolen. An instant scan of passport numbers will disclose whether the passport was reported stolen or was connected with the commission of a crime.

Regardless of its role in combating terrorism, Interpol is still an organization that helps to solve crime on the local level every day. An important task for the future is to make sure that police forces around the world are aware of Interpol's capabilities and how to put them to use. Continuous education is important.

When he was elected secretary-general, Noble noted: "Interpol must never forget that its client is the rank and file police officer, who

Should the United States Belong? Ronald Noble Answers

Some people think that the United States should not belong to an organization in which nations that support terrorists—such as Iraq, Yemen, and Syria—are equal partners. But Ronald Noble thinks that such a situation is a strength of Interpol. "If you're looking for dangerous people," he says, "you don't care whether it's your enemy or your friend who tells you, as long as you find out."

Many American law-enforcement people don't want to share information they have acquired with other countries. They're afraid it will get into the hands of the wrong people. Noble thinks that Americans have "a long-held feeling that we can only trust ourselves."

in the twenty-first century must pursue criminals who often have the upper hand in technology and resources and operate in an increasingly borderless world."

While helping the local police officer, Interpol also has to be a player on the international stage. That may not have been possible in past decades, but Secretary-General Ronald Kendall said of his fifteen years in office, "When I started, if I visited a country, I never got to see the interior minister or somebody at that upper level. Recognition for Interpol is something I've struggled for, to get some recognition at the political level."

In June 1998, Kendall delivered a speech to the United Nations General Assembly in New York. Invitations to speak before the General Assembly are usually reserved for heads of nations. Clearly, Interpol has gained a great deal of international respect in recent years. The organization's new emphasis on technology and its equal treatment of all nations, regardless of their politics, allow it to follow its own mission statement. Interpol will increase the respect—and usefulness—it earns in the future.

Interpol's Mission Statement

To be the world's preeminent police organization in support of all organizations, authorities and services whose mission is preventing, detecting, and suppressing crime. We will achieve this by:
- Providing both a global perspective and a regional focus
- Exchanging information that is timely, accurate, relevant and complete
- Facilitating international cooperation
- Coordinating joint operational activities of our member countries
- Making available know-how, expertise, and good practice

We will act on the basis of the articulated demands and expectations of these organizations, authorities and services, while remaining alert to developments so as to be able to anticipate future requirements.

Time Line

1809 Paris police begin a detective bureau under former criminal François Vidocq.
1914 Prince Albert I of Monaco organizes First International Criminal Police Conference, but war intervenes.
1923 Dr. Johann Schober of Austria restarts the organization. The headquarters of the International Criminal Police Commission is in Vienna.
1929 The League of Nations recognizes the ICPC's authority in matters of counterfeit currency.
1938 Germany takes over the ICPC headquarters in Vienna and moves it to Berlin. Other countries resign their membership.
1945 Police officers from throughout Europe revive the international criminal police.
1950 J. Edgar Hoover pulls the United States out of Interpol as the result of a political argument.
1955 ICPC's General Assembly establishes National Central Bureaus.
1956 The organization's name is officially changed to International Criminal Police Organization (Interpol).
1966 Interpol moves out of Paris to the suburb of St. Cloud.
1969 The United States opens a National Central Bureau in Washington, D.C.
1984 The General Assembly votes to begin considering terrorist acts as crimes rather than political acts.
1985 The General Assembly elects Raymond E. Kendall, the first non-Frenchman to be secretary general.
1989 Interpol moves into new, secure headquarters in the French city of Lyon.
1999 Project Bridge is started to fight against the smuggling of people.
2000 American Ronald K. Noble becomes secretary-general.
2002 Most nations are networked to Interpol by computer. Parts of the Interpol web site become available to the public.

Glossary

bureaucracy nonelected government officials

capital punishment putting a criminal to death as a result of a trial and judgment

cartel a combination of various businesses that join to eliminate competition from other businesses

counterfeit to make a fake version of something valuable, hoping others will think it is real

domestic happening at home

drug trafficking the entire illegal business of selling, moving, and distributing illegal drugs

extortion obtaining money or property from someone by force or other illegal means

forger someone who makes fake or false documents

fraud deception or misrepresentation

globalized spread or distributed throughout the world

heroin a powdery white illegal drug derived from opium

hijack to steal a vehicle with people in it

money laundering moving money around internationally in order to hide where it originally came from

multinational involving more than one nation

prostitution engaging in sexual activity for money

ransom the payment requested in exchange for releasing something or someone

terrorist a nongovernment organization or individual who carries out violence in order to force a change

treaty an official agreement between countries that defines what can and cannot be done in a specific situation

warrant official authorization to make an arrest or search private premises

To Find Out More

BOOKS

Bayer, Linda N. *Drugs, Crime, and Criminal Justice*. Crime, Justice, and Punishment Series. Chelsea House Publishers, 2001.

DeAngelis, Gina. *Cyber Crimes*. Crime, Justice, and Punishment Series. Chelsea House Publishers, 2000.

Fridell, Ron. *DNA Fingerprinting: The Ultimate Identity*. Franklin Watts, 2001.

Lane, Brian. *Eyewitness: Crime and Detection*. DK Publishing, 2000.

Roden, Katie. *Solving International Crime*. Crimebusters Series. Copper Beech Books, 1996.

Tocci, Salvatore. *High-Tech IDs: From Finger Scans to Voice Patterns*. Franklin Watts, 2000.

Stewart, Gail, editor. *The Death Penalty: Opposing Viewpoints*. Opposing Viewpoints Series. Greenhaven Press, 1998.

ADDRESSES AND WEB SITES

INTERPOL
General Secretariat
200, quai Charles de Gaulle
69006 Lyon
France
www.interpol.int/

U.S. National Central Bureau
Department of Justice
Washington, D.C. 20530-0001
(202) 616-9000
www.usdoj.gov/usncb/

Index

Achille Lauro 33-34
Albert I, Prince 8
Al-Qaeda 22
Arab Interior Ministers' Council 17
Article 3 13, 34
art theft 36-37
Austria 9, 11
Automatic Fingerprint Identification System 25

Belgium 11
bin Laden, Osama 20, 21, 22
biometrics 25, 26

capital punishment 41
Carlos the Jackal 32
car theft 20, 35
China 9
CITES 17, 18
codes 12, 24
computers 24, 26-27
constitution 11, 14, 34
counterfeit money 10, 39
crime, domestic 6
 international 7
Czechoslovakia 31

database 4, 20, 28-29, 30
de Guzman, Onel 40
Denmark 4
detectives 8
DNA identification 26
Dressler, Dr. Oskar 9
drug cartel 35
drugs, heroin 4
 opium 5
drug trafficking 4, 5, 35
Ducloux, Louis 11

Einhorn, Ira 41-42
Espigares Mira, Jesus 15
Executive Committee 14-15
extradition 20, 41

facsimile 24
Faurot, Joseph 8
Federal Bureau of Investigation (FBI) 11, 18, 31

fingerprinting 8, 25, 26
forgery 6, 7
France 8
fraud 30

General Assembly 10, 12, 13, 14, 18, 34
General Regulations 14
General Secretariat 16, 18
Germany 10

Henry, Sir Edward 8
heroin 4
Hitler, Adolf 10-11
Hoover, J. Edgar 11, 18, 31

illegal immigration 37-38
information on criminals 6, 29
International Criminal Information System 28
International Criminal Police Commission 9
International Criminal Police Conference 8-9
Internet 29, 40
Interpol, founding 9
 headquarters 11, 12, 13, 14
 mission 44
 origin of name 12
 structure 16
iris identification 26

Japan 9

Kendall, Raymond 13, 18, 44
kidnapping 17
Klinghoffer, Leon 33
Kyrgystan 20

League of Nations 10
Libya 22, 32
Lyon, France 12, 14, 16, 17

Millennium Project 35
missing persons 23
money laundering 15, 35, 36
Monaco 8

National Central Bureau (NCB) 12, 16, 17-19, 20

Nazis 10
Nevitt, Peter 5, 26-27
Nigeria 4
Noble, Ronald K. 15, 16, 27, 34, 37, 42, 43
notices 20, 21, 22-24, 31, 41

Organization of Petroleum Exporting Countries 32
organized crime 35

people smuggling 37-39
Popular Front for the Liberation of Palestine 32, 33
Project Bridge 39

radio 10
Reemstma, Jan Philipp 17

St. Cloud, France 12, 13
Scotland Yard 8, 13
secretary-general 9, 15, 18
Schober, Dr. Johann 9
Simpson, John 15
Singapore 4
smuggling 37, 38
Soviet Union 9
Spain 15, 17
Sûreté 8, 11
Sweden 23
Switzerland 11

telegraph 10, 24
teletypewriter 10, 24
terrorism 7, 12, 13, 31-33, 42-44

United Kingdom 8, 11, 13,
United States National Central Bureau (USNCB) 19
Universal Declaration of Human Rights 6, 13

Vidocq, François 8

Washington, D.C. 15
wildlife crime 18
World Trade Center 34
World Wide Web 29